English
made easy

Key Stage 2
Ages 8-9

Author John Hesk
Consultant Claire White

Certificate

Congratulations to ...
(write your name here)
for successfully finishing this book.

☆ *You're a star!* ☆

Fact or fantasy?

Carefully read the **question** below and the seven **statements** that relate to it.

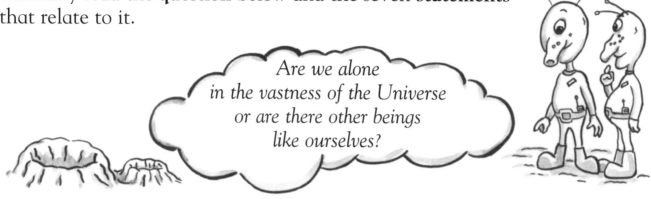

Are we alone in the vastness of the Universe or are there other beings like ourselves?

1   This is a <u>question</u> that has long fascinated scientists and fired the imagination of writers, artists and filmmakers.

2   In the Middle Ages, people believed that the Earth was at the centre of the Universe. They thought that the Sun moved around the Earth.

3   We now know that the Sun is at the centre of our Solar System and that we, together with eight (or possibly nine!) other worlds, are moving around it. We also realise that our Sun is just one of at least 100,000 million stars in the Galaxy, and that there are millions of other such galaxies out there somewhere!

4   It is certainly possible that parallel universes with inhabited planets do exist. Yet, until we develop the ability to travel at what now seem like impossible speeds, we shall not be able to visit them.

5   This does not necessarily mean that others, more technologically advanced than humans, are not, at this very moment, on their way to find us.

6   Many people believe that they have seen spacecraft from other worlds. Some even claim to have met alien beings from these unknown galaxies. Can some of these so-called "close encounters" be real, or are they all purely imaginary?

7   There is still so much to learn before we can know the whole truth.

Reread the statements, underlining all the **key words**.

The main points

Reread *Fact or fantasy?* on page 2. Make brief **notes** on the **main points** in each statement.

1 ....

   ....

2 ....

   ....

3 ....

   ....

4 ....

   ....

5 ....

   ....

6 ....

   ....

7 ....

   ....

Word-building

Look carefully at the changes in these **words**.

    take – taking
    hope – hopeful
    love – lovely
    try – trying
    try – tries

Now complete this **spelling guide**.

When a word has a silent **-e** at the end, it usually loses this **-e** when we add .... but keeps it when we add .... or ....

Before adding an **-s** to words that end in a **consonant** followed by **-y**, change the .... to ....

Add **-ing** to these words. D

make + **-ing** becomes ....   flame + **-ing** becomes ....

move + **-ing** becomes ....   phone + **-ing** becomes ....

save + **-ing** becomes ....   dance + **-ing** becomes ....

Add **-ful** to these words. D

hope + **-ful** becomes ....   grace + **-ful** becomes ....

hate + **-ful** becomes ....   care + **-ful** becomes ....

use + **-ful** becomes ....   taste + **-ful** becomes ....

Add an **-s** to these words. Change the **-y** only if you need to. D

fly + **-s** becomes ....   dry + **-s** becomes ....

cry + **-s** becomes ....   multiply + **-s** becomes ....

carry + **-s** becomes ....   key + **-s** becomes ....

fry + **-s** becomes ....   assembly + **-s** becomes ....

Now write some **-ing**, **-ful** and **-s** words of your own. D

.... + **-ing** becomes .... + **-ing** becomes ....

.... + **-ful** becomes .... + **-ful** becomes ....

.... + **-s** becomes .... + **-s** becomes ....

More word-building

Do you know this verse?
> **i** *before* **e**,
> *Except after* **c**,
> *When the sound is* **ee**.

The words below follow this rule. Write the full word.

rec__ __ve ....

dec__ __ve ....

c__ __ling ....

f__ __ld ....

n__ __ce ....

p__ __r ....

ch__ __f ....

th__ __f ....

These words break the rule, so check in a **dictionary** before you write them. D

s__ __ze ....

w__ __rd ....

spec__ __s ....

Match the following **prefixes** and **root words** to make new words. Then include each new word in a sentence.

Remember: A **prefix** is a group of letters added to the beginning of a word.

prefixes	roots
in	regular
im	tect
ir	pend
pro	prove
sus	vent

....

....

....

....

....

....

....

....

....

Dictionary work

Look up the following words in a **dictionary**, then write a short **definition**, or meaning, for each word. D

advent ....

invent ....

prevent ....

cycle ....

bicycle ....

tricycle ....

telephone ....

microphone ....

earphone ....

real ....

realise ....

unreal ....

Write the **root words** for each group of words above.
Remember: A **root word** is a word that can have other letters (prefixes and suffixes) added to it.

....

Now create a new word from each of the **root words** below by adding letters.

scope ....   graph ....

medic ....   press ....

Split suffixes

-ible   -able   -ive   -ion

Make as many real words as you can by adding the **suffixes** above to the list below. Don't forget to check your spelling in a **dictionary** before you write the word! D

Remember: A **suffix** is a group of letters added to the end of a word.

collect ....

nat ....

respons ....

sens ....

port ....

Now write three more words ending with each **suffix**.

-ible ....

-able ....

-ive ....

-ion ....

Remember: Add any new words to your **word bank**.

More on plurals

Complete the following rules.

How to make plurals

1 For most **nouns**, simply add ....

2 If the **noun** ends with **-s**, **-sh** or **-ch**, add ....

3 For most **nouns** ending with an **-f**, change the **f** to ...., and then add.......... .

4 If the **noun** ends with **-ly**, **-ry** or **-ty**, change the .... to ...., and then add ....

5 If the **noun ends** with **-ay**, **-ey**, **-oy**, just add.......... .

Find examples of **nouns** that end in each of the ways described above.
Write the words as both **singular** and **plural** nouns.
Remember: A **noun** is a naming word.

1..

2..

3 ....

4 ....

5 ....

Peculiar plurals!
Add **-es** to these words.

potato ....   echo ....   tomato ....

Add only **-s** to these words.

solo ....   photo ....   piano ....

Zulu ....   banana ....   kiwi ....

Big, bigger, biggest

Look below to see how we change the "amount" that an **adjective** expresses.

Big is an **adjective**.

Bigger is a **comparative** adjective.
It is used to **compare** two things.

Biggest is a **superlative** adjective.
It is used when **comparing** three or more things.

Complete the pattern in this table.

Adjective	Comparative	Superlative
old	older	oldest
young		
soon		
late		
quick		
slow		

Now try these – but be careful! D

Adjective	Comparative	Superlative
good		
many		

9

Tricky words

Rewrite the sentences below, choosing the right word from the brackets.
Remember: **It's** with an apostrophe is the shortened form of **it is**.
Its without an apostrophe means that something **belongs to it**.

[It's/its] time to give the dog [it's/its] dinner.

....

....

When [it's/its] likely to rain, [it's/its] best to take
an umbrella.

....

....

Before riding your bicycle, [it's/its] a good idea
to check [it's/its] brakes.

....

....

Remember: **They're** with an apostrophe is the shortened form of **they are**.
Their means that something **belongs to them**.
There indicates **position**.

[They're/their/there] going to shops to buy [they're/their/there] clothes.

....

....

Write a sentence of your own using **their** and another sentence using **they're**.

....

....

Punctuation practice

Name these **punctuation marks**.

, ...   : ....

; ....   - ....

" ....   ! ....

Now rewrite the text below, **punctuating** it correctly and breaking it into **paragraphs**.

giants have been the main characters in fairy tales myths and legends for centuries they have been imaginary figures of fear and fun throughout the world from the west to the east and from the north pole to the south pole some have strange names like polyphemus the cyclops from greece blunderbore from england and jotun from scandinavia in many traditional stories giants who smell trouble will often thunder fee fi fo fum they are not always very clever so small cunning heroes can trick them and escape from their clutches

....

....

....

....

....

....

....

....

....

Reading and understanding

Read the text below, then answer the questions in **full sentences**.

People used to believe that in ancient times Great Britain was populated by a race of giants. In legendary tales, giants are sometimes linked with particular places. Some stories about giants were originally told to explain how certain features of the landscape came to exist.

In Northern Ireland, an amazing formation of thousands of columns of basalt, an igneous rock, is known as The Giant's Causeway.

Some people think that the Gog Magog Hills in Cambridgeshire, England, take their name from two legendary giants, Gog and Magog, who were said to be buried in the area.

Another story tells how The Wrekin, a hill in another part of England, was first formed when an angry giant cast down a huge spadeful of rocks and soil.

Why did people tell stories about giants?

....

....

Where is The Giant's Causeway?

....

....

How might the Gog Magog Hills have got their name?

....

....

What is the Wrekin?

....

....

Which of these places would you like to visit, and why?

....

....

Silent w

In the passage about giants on page 12, the hill called The Wrekin has a silent **w**. All the words below also begin with a silent **w**. Add the missing letters, then use each word in a sentence of your own. D

__ __estle   __ __iting   __ __iggle

__ __en   __ __ing   __ __ong

__ __inkle   __ __eath   __ __ote

....

....

....

....

....

....

....

....

Do you know or can you find any more words that begin with **wr-**?
Make a list here. D

....

....

....

....

A traditional story

Many **myths**, **legends** and **traditional stories** from around the world are about such things as fire, water, rain, wind or thunder and lightning. Sometimes these things take the form of giants, gods or spirits that can harm or help humans. Carefully read the following **information** about Norse gods.

Thor and Sif

What Thor was like

Thor was an exaggerated, colourful character. He was huge, even for a god, and incredibly strong. He had wild hair and beard and a temper to match. He was never angry for long, though, and easily forgave people. Thor raced across the sky in his chariot drawn by two giant goats, **Toothgnasher** and **Toothgrinder**. It was their hooves that people heard when it thundered on Earth. He controlled the thunder and lightning and brewed up storms by blowing through his beard. Sailors prayed to him for protection from bad weather.

Thor's magic weapons

Thor had a belt which doubled his strength when he buckled it on and iron gauntlets which allowed him to grasp any weapon. The most famous of Thor's weapons was his hammer, **Mjollnir**. It always hit its target and returned to Thor's hands after use. When a thunderbolt struck Earth, people said that Thor had flung down his hammer.

Mjollnir did not only do harm, though. It also had protective powers and people wore small copies of it as jewellery to keep them safe and bring good luck.

Sif

Thor was married to **Sif**, who was famous for her pure gold, flowing hair. She was a goddess of fruitfulness and plenty. Her hair reminded people of a field of ripe corn and the harvest.

In one of the myths her hair was cut and stolen. Her misery until the hair was replaced represented the darkness of the winter season, when the corn did not grow.

Sif and Thor lived in a great hall in Asgard, called **Bilskirnir**, which means Lightning.

From *The Usborne Book of Greek and Norse Legends*

Underline any words in the **extract** above that you do not understand, then look up their meanings in a dictionary. D

Understanding the story

Use **full sentences** to answer these questions about the **information** on page 14.

How did the Norse people explain the sound of thunder?

....

....

What did the people say had happened when lightning struck Earth?

....

....

What happened on Earth when Thor blew through his beard?

....

....

Why did the Norse sailors pray to Thor?

....

....

What was magical about Thor's belt and gloves?

....

....

Why were copies of Mjollnir worn as jewellery?

....

....

Why was Sif famous?

....

....

What did Sif's unhappiness at the loss of her hair represent?

....

....

An Aboriginal myth

The Aboriginal people of Australia have stories about thunder and lightning. Read the two **myths** below about thunderstorms, and answer the questions that follow.

Thunderstorms

On Melville Island it is a woman, Bumerali, who strikes the ground with her stone axes mounted on long flexible handles. These are the lightning flashes which destroy the trees and sometimes the Aborigines.

The Arnhem Land Aborigines believe that the thunder-man, Jambuwul, travels from place to place on the large cumulus clouds of the wet season, shedding the life-giving rain on the earth beneath. These thunder-clouds are also the home of tiny spirit children, the yurtus, who travel on the raindrops to descend to earth and find a human mother.

From *Dreamtime Heritage* by A. and M. J. Roberts

How does Bumerali make lightning?

....

....

Who is Jambuwul?

....

....

What are the yurtus?

....

....

Another Aboriginal myth

Read this Aboriginal **myth** about fire, and answer the questions that follow.

The Capture of Fire

Goodah, a noted magician, captured a piece of lightning as it struck a dead tree during a storm. He imprisoned it as a convenient way to make fire for his own use, and ignored demands that he share this wonderful discovery. At last the tribe became so enraged with Goodah that a group of elders called up a whirlwind just as Goodah had made a fire with his piece of lightning. The whirlwind picked up the fire and scattered it all over the country, and fire became common property when members of the tribe picked up enough burning wood to make fires for themselves.

To escape the jeers and laughter of the tribe, Goodah fled to the hills to sulk, and to plan revenge.

From *Dreamtime Heritage* by A. and M. J. Roberts

How would you describe Goodah's behaviour?

....

....

....

What does **common property** mean?

....

....

....

Do you think Goodah was right to feel angry with the tribe for calling up a whirlwind?

....

....

A scientific explanation

Here is a **scientific description** of the causes of thunder and lightning.

Thunder and Lightning

Thunderclouds are huge and awesomely powerful. Very big thunderclouds tower 16 km (10 miles) or more into the air and contain enough energy to light a small town for a year. No wonder then, that they can unleash such devastating storms.

It takes very strong updraughts of air to build such huge and powerful clouds, which is why they tend to form along "cold fronts", or over ground heated by strong sunshine. Violent air currents sweep up and down outside the cloud, tearing the water droplets and ice crystals apart and then crashing them together again. These collisions load the cloud particles with static electricity – just as rubbing a balloon on a pullover does. Lightning is the sudden release of the charge built up on millions of particles within the thundercloud.

A flash of lightning heats the air along its path so dramatically that it expands at supersonic speed. This expansion causes a deafening crash of thunder.

From *How the Earth Works* by John Farndon

How is static electricity formed in clouds?

....

....

....

What happens when static electricity is released?

....

Find words that could be used in *Thunder and Lightning* in place of the words below. T D

huge .... awesomely ....

unleash .... deafening ....

Types of writing

Reread the **information** about Thor and Sif on page 14, the Australian Aboriginal **myths** on pages 16 and 17, and the modern **scientific explanation** of thunder and lightning on page 18. Then place the following numbered statements under the correct headings below.

1 Lightning is the release of static electricity.
2 Thunderclouds can be more than 16 km (10 miles) high.
3 Lightning is Thor's hammer.
4 Thunder is the sound of giant goats' hooves in the sky.
5 Thunder is the sound of rapidly heating air expanding.
6 Thunder comes from the thunder-man, who travels on the clouds.
7 Rain gives life to things on earth.
8 Raindrops carry tiny spirits.
9 Devastating storms often accompany thunder and lightning.
10 Thor brews up storms by blowing through his beard.
11 Fire is precious to humans.
12 Selfish behaviour is bad.
13 Sharing with others is good.

Norse legend	**Aboriginal myths**	**Scientific explanation**
Statement 3		

Planning your own story

Reread the **myth** on page 17. On a separate sheet of paper, write notes on how Goodah found fire. Decide what Goodah did next. How will you end the story? Plan your story on this page by writing short notes. Decide who you will be writing your story for.

Remember: You do not need to use full sentences when writing notes.

Characters: ....

....

Setting: ....

Beginning: ....

....

....

What happens: ....

....

....

....

....

....

....

Ending: ....

....

....

Your own traditional tale

Look over the notes you wrote on page 20, then write your story here.
Remember: Use **paragraphs** for each different idea.

The Capture of Fire, and Goodah's Revenge

....

....

....

....

....

....

....

....

....

....

....

....

....

....

Patterns in poems

Read the following **poem** aloud, then answer the questions.

Who has seen the wind?
   Neither I nor you:
But when the leaves hang trembling
   The wind is passing thro'.

Who has seen the wind?
   Neither you nor I:
But when the trees bow down their heads
   The wind is passing by.

Christina Rossetti

How many **verses** (or stanzas) are there in this poem?

....

Find the **rhyming pairs** of words in the poem. Write them here.

....

Read aloud the poem, listen to the **rhythm** and count the **syllables**.
Write the number of **syllables** in each line of the poem here.

line 1 ....   line 2 ....   line 3 ....   line 4 ....

line 5 ....   line 6 ....   line 7 ....   line 8 ....

Write your own poem about another type of weather in the same style.

....

....

....

Haiku and cinquain

Read these two **poems** aloud.

Haiku
Poem in three lines:
Five syllables, then seven,
Five again; no rhyme.

Eric Finney

Cinquain
Cinquain:
A short verse form
Of counted syllables …
And first devised by Adelaide
Crapsey.

Gerard Benson

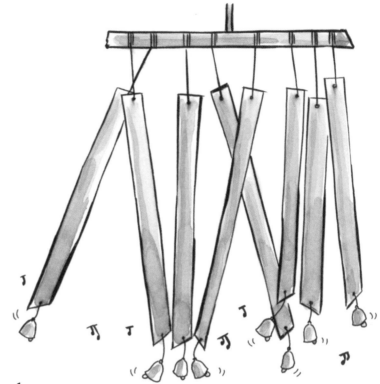

Write your own **haiku** about wind.
Remember to use the correct number of **syllables** in each line.

Wind

syllables: 5 ....

             7 ....

             5 ....

Now write a **cinquain**. Use the same number of **syllables** in each line as
in the **cinquain** above.

Wind

syllables: 2 ....

             4 ....

             6 ....

             8 ....

             2 ....

Soft c and homophones

All the **definitions** below are of words that begin with **ci-**. The letter **c** sounds like an **s** when these words are spoken. Use a **dictionary** to help you find the words that fit the **definitions**. D

a drink made from apples ....

a partly burned fuel such as coal ....

a character in a fairy tale ....

where films are shown ....

a spice ....

a shape ....

the distance round a circle ....

a travelling show ....

a large town ....

polite ....

The words below sound the same, but are spelt differently and have different meanings. They are called **homophones**.

great and grate   paws, pores and pause   rain, rein and reign

Can you find a **homophone** for each of these words?

awe   ....   bear ....

ceiling...............................   draft ....

eight   ....   fare ....

guest   ....   hare ....

inn   ....   bye ....

wait   ....   sea ....

pare   ....   feet ....

24

Protest letter

Read this **letter** from the *Letters to the Editor* section of a local **newspaper**, then answer, in **full sentences**, the following questions.

> Sir,
>
> I wish to protest, on behalf of the B.B.G. (Ban the By-pass Group), about the proposed building of a road through Birnam Wood, which was reported in last Friday's *Dunsinane Express*.
>
> The loss to the public of this local beauty spot and the damage to the wildlife that depends upon it would be huge.
>
> The wood has been allowed to grow and flourish, largely undisturbed by man, for almost one thousand years.
>
> Surely we, as local guardians of the environment, cannot allow the road builders to destroy this priceless piece of our natural history?
>
> M. Duncan (address supplied)

Why was this **letter** written?

....

....

In which **paragraphs** does the writer give reasons for his protest? What are his reasons?

....

....

....

Why does the writer end with a **question**?

....

....

Do you think this **letter** will help stop the wood from being destroyed? If yes, how? If no, why not?

....

....

Plan an argument

Do you support or disagree with the letter on page 25? Gather together some **facts**, **opinions** and **persuasive** words so that you can plan your own **letter**. It may help to look in **reference books,** or on the **Internet**. Make some **notes** here.

Facts about trees and the environment

....

....

....

....

....

My opinion and feelings

....

....

....

....

Useful words to persuade people ☐D ☐T

Greed, devastation, ...

....

....

....

....

Letter to the newspaper

Read over your **notes** on page 26, then write your own **letter** to the newspaper about the by-pass discussed on page 25.

(your address)

....

....

(date)

....

The Editor
Dunsinane Express.

Dear Sir,

....

....

....

....

....

....

....

....

....

Yours faithfully,

....

Write an explanation

Imagine that you have to **explain** what a banana is and where it comes from to someone who has never seen or heard of one. Write your **explanation** below. You may need to find out a few extra **facts** before you begin. D

....

....

....

....

....

....

....

....

....

....

....

After you have written your **explanation**, turn this page
upside down, and check whether your **explanation**
includes any of the information given below.

A banana is an edible tropical fruit. It is finger-shaped and has a yellow skin when ripe. We usually peel off the skin and eat the pulpy inside, which is creamy white in colour.
Bananas grow in clusters on tree-like plants. They are grown in Africa, Asia, the West Indies and Latin America and are exported all over the world.

Instructions

A banana split is a dessert made with ice cream and a split banana. Other ingredients may be added as decoration. Write **instructions** for making a banana split. (You may need to look them up in a recipe book.) These words may be useful: peel, half/halved, lengthways, pile, decorate. **Remember**: Begin with an **introduction** that lists the ingredients, and then continue with short, **numbered statements** in the right order. D

Make a point

Here is a list of ideas for a piece of **writing** about travel in towns and cities.

Improved public transport would make our towns and cities safer places.
Travel in towns and cities is sometimes slow and difficult.
Pedestrians and cyclists have to breathe polluted air.
Public transport reduces air pollution.
Private cars carry only a few people.
Buses and trains can carry many people.
Many towns and cities are too noisy and dirty.
Cars carrying a few people can cause traffic jams.
Walking and cycling are good exercise.
Public transport saves fuel.

Sort these **points** into a sensible order by giving each one a number. Then use the **points** to write one or two **paragraphs** about travel in towns and cities.

....

....

....

....

....

....

....

....

....

....

....

Onomatopoeia

The words below have **sounds** that match their meanings.
Remember: When the sound of a word connects with its meaning, it is called **onomatopoeic**.

splash   crash   smash   clash

clatter   plop   clap

gurgle   snap   buzz   rumble

tinkle   click   whir   tick

bang   roar   squeal

Match the **sound words** above to the different situations below. Write the relevant **sound word** in the appropriate box. Add some more **sound words** of your own if you wish!

Thunderstorm *crash* ....
....

Sports day ....
....

In the swimming pool ....
....

In the kitchen ....
....

Word game

Follow the rules below to make as many words as you can from the word **TRANSPORT**.

Follow these rules:

- for each word that you make, you can use a letter as many times as it appears in the word **TRANSPORT**. This means that you can use **T** and **R** twice in a word, but all the other letters only once

- words of **fewer than three letters** do not count

- **names** of people and places do not count

- each word must be in a **dictionary** D

- each word scores **one point**

....

....

....

....

....

....

....

....

Total points ....

(15–20 good, 20–25 very good, over 25 excellent!)

Answer Section with Parents' Notes

Key Stage 2
Ages 8–9

This 8-page section provides answers or explanatory notes to all the activities in this book. This will enable you to assess your child's work.

Point out any spelling mistakes, incorrect punctuation and grammatical errors as you mark each page. Also correct any handwriting errors. (Your child should use the handwriting style taught at his or her school.) As well as making corrections, it is very important to praise your child's efforts and achievements.

Encourage your child to use a dictionary, and suggest that he or she uses a notebook to compile a **word bank** of new words or difficult spellings.

Fact or fantasy?

Carefully read the **question** below and the seven **statements** that relate to it.

Are we alone in the vastness of the Universe or are there other beings like ourselves?

1 This is a <u>question</u> that has long fascinated scientists and fired the imagination of writers, artists and filmmakers.

2 In the Middle Ages, people believed that the Earth was at the centre of the Universe. They thought that the Sun moved around the Earth.

3 We now know that the Sun is at the centre of our Solar System and that we, together with eight (or possibly nine!) other worlds, are moving around it. We also realise that our Sun is just one of at least 100,000 million stars in the Galaxy, and that there are millions of other such galaxies out there somewhere!

4 It is certainly possible that parallel universes with inhabited planets do exist. Yet, until we develop the ability to travel at what now seem like impossible speeds, we shall not be able to visit them.

5 This does not necessarily mean that others, more technologically advanced than humans, are not, at this very moment, on their way to find us.

6 Many people believe that they have seen spacecraft from other worlds. Some even claim to have met alien beings from these unknown galaxies. Can some of these so-called "close encounters" be real, or are they all purely imaginary?

7 There is still so much to learn before we can know the whole truth.

Reread the statements, underlining all the **key words**.

This page sets out seven non-fiction statements, which your child reads to gather specific information. By underlining key words, your child will be practising the skills needed to sort important facts from other text, as well as improving his or her comprehension.

The main points

Reread *Fact or fantasy?* on page 2. Make brief **notes** on the **main points** in each statement.

1 ....
2 ....
3 ....
4 ....
5 ....
6 ....
7 ....

Your child should use the key words underlined on page 2 to help with this exercise. Check that he or she has noted the most important facts from each of the statements. The notes should be brief and need not be written in full sentences.

Word-building

Look carefully at the changes in these **words**.
take – taking
hope – hopeful
love – lovely
try – trying
try – tries

Now complete this **spelling guide**.

When a word has a silent **-e** at the end, it usually loses this **-e** when we add ....**ing**.... but keeps it when we add ....**ful**.... or ....**ly**.... .

Before adding an **-s** to words that end in a **consonant** followed by **-y**, change the ....**y**.... to ....**ie**.... .

Add **-ing** to these words. [D]

make + **-ing** becomes	making	flame + **-ing** becomes	flaming
move + **-ing** becomes	moving	phone + **-ing** becomes	phoning
save + **-ing** becomes	saving	dance + **-ing** becomes	dancing

Add **-ful** to these words. [D]

hope + **-ful** becomes	hopeful	grace + **-ful** becomes	graceful
hate + **-ful** becomes	hateful	care + **-ful** becomes	careful
use + **-ful** becomes	useful	taste + **-ful** becomes	tasteful

Add an **-s** to these words. Change the **-y** only if you need to. [D]

fly + **-s** becomes	flies	dry + **-s** becomes	dries
cry + **-s** becomes	cries	multiply + **-s** becomes	multiplies
carry + **-s** becomes	carries	key + **-s** becomes	keys
fry + **-s** becomes	fries	assembly + **-s** becomes	assemblies

Now write some **-ing**, **-ful** and **-s** words of your own. [D]

.... + **-ing** becomes .... + **-ing** becomes ....
.... + **-ful** becomes .... + **-ful** becomes ....
.... + **-s** becomes .... + **-s** becomes ....

This page uses word-building as an aid to spelling. Make sure that your child has completed and understood the two rules at the top of the page before he or she begins the exercises below. Encourage your child to check his or her answers in a dictionary.

More word-building

Do you know this verse?
i before e,
Except after c,
When the sound is ee.

The words below follow this rule. Write the full word.

rec__ __ve .... receive   n__ __ce .... niece

dec__ __ve .... deceive   p__ __r .... pier

c__ __ling .... ceiling   ch__ __f .... chief

f__ __ld .... field   th__ __f .... thief

These words break the rule, so check in a **dictionary** before you write them. D

s__ __ze .... seize

w__ __rd .... weird

spec__ __s .... species

Match the following **prefixes** and **root words** to make new words. Then include each new word in a sentence.
Remember: A **prefix** is a group of letters added to the beginning of a word.

prefixes	roots
in	regular
im	tect
ir	pend
pro	prove
sus	vent

invent
improve
irregular
protect
suspend

....
....
....
Answers may vary

Check that your child knows and understands the verse. Use the word *chief* to show that the rule applies to the ee sound only when it immediately follows *c*. Learning the meanings of common prefixes and roots will also improve your child's spelling.

Dictionary work

Look up the following words in a **dictionary**, then write a short **definition**, or meaning, for each word. D

advent   an arrival

invent   to make or create

prevent   to stop something

cycle   a repeating chain of events

bicycle   a vehicle with two wheels

tricycle   a vehicle with three wheels

telephone   a device for talking to someone far away

microphone   a device for making sounds heard further away

earphone   a device for carrying sound to the ear

real   existing

realise   to become aware

unreal   not existing

Write the **root words** for each group of words above.
Remember: A **root word** is a word that can have other letters (prefixes and suffixes) added to it.

vent   cycle   phone   real

Now create a new word from each of the **root words** below by adding letters.

scope   microscope   graph   photograph

medic   medical   press   express

This page focuses on root words in order to improve spelling skills and provide practice in using a dictionary. Explain that the meaning of each root word is always the same within a group of words – for example, *scope* is always to do with *seeing*.

Split suffixes

-ible   -able   -ive   -ion

Make as many real words as you can by adding the **suffixes** above to the list below. Don't forget to check your spelling in a **dictionary** before you write the word! D
Remember: A **suffix** is a group of letters added to the end of a word.

collect   collectable (or collectible), collective, collection

nat   native, nation

respons   responsible, responsive

sens   sensible

port   portable, portion

Now write three more words ending with each **suffix**.

-ible   ....

-able   ....

-ive   ....

-ion   ....

Remember: Add any new words to your **word bank**.

Here the task is to make new words by adding suffixes to some roots, which are not always words in their own right. This will help to extend your child's vocabulary and provide spelling practice. Ensure that your child checks any words in a dictionary.

More on plurals

Complete the following rules.

How to make plurals

1 For most **nouns**, simply add ....s.... .

2 If the **noun** ends with -s, -sh or -ch, add ....es.... .

3 For most **nouns** ending with an -f, change the f to ....v...., and then add ....es.... .

4 If the **noun** ends with -ly, -ry or -ty, change the ....y.... to ....ie...., and then add ....s.... .

5 If the **noun** ends with -ay, -ey, -oy, just add ....s.... .

Find examples of **nouns** that end in each of the ways described above. Write the words as both **singular** and **plural** nouns.
Remember: A **noun** is a naming word.

1 ....
2 ....
3 ....
4 ....
5 ....

Peculiar plurals!
Add **-es** to these words.

potato   potatoes   echo   echoes   tomato   tomatoes

Add only **-s** to these words.

solo   solos   photo photos   piano   pianos

Zulu   Zulus   banana bananas   kiwi   kiwis

This page focuses on five general rules that will help your child to form plurals. The final activity features a number of common words that do not follow these rules.

Big, bigger, biggest

Look below to see how we change the "amount" that an **adjective** expresses.

Big is an **adjective**.

Bigger is a **comparative** adjective.
It is used to **compare** two things.

Biggest is a **superlative** adjective.
It is used when **comparing** three or more things.

Complete the pattern in this table.

Adjective	Comparative	Superlative
old	older	oldest
young	younger	youngest
soon	sooner	soonest
late	later	latest
quick	quicker	quickest
slow	slower	slowest

Now try these – but be careful! D

Adjective	Comparative	Superlative
good	better	best
many	more	most

In this activity your child is asked to list the comparative and superlative forms of common adjectives. Point out that although the root words change in the last two exercises, they are still examples of comparative and superlative adjectives.

Tricky words

Rewrite the sentences below, choosing the right word from the brackets.
Remember: **It's** with an apostrophe is the shortened form of **it is**.
Its without an apostrophe means that something **belongs to it**.

[It's/its] time to give the dog [it's/its] dinner.
It's time to give the dog its dinner.

When [it's/its] likely to rain, [it's/its] best to take an umbrella.
When it's likely to rain, it's best to take an umbrella.

Before riding your bicycle, [it's/its] a good idea to check [it's/its] brakes.
Before riding your bicycle, it's a good idea to check its brakes.

Remember: **They're** with an apostrophe is the shortened form of **they are**.
Their means that something **belongs to them**.
There indicates **position**.

[They're/their/there] going to shops to buy [they're/their/there] clothes.
They're going to shops to buy their clothes.

Write a sentence of your own using **their** and another sentence using **they're**.
Answers may vary

This activity provides practice in the correct usage of *its* and *it's*, and *they're*, *their* and *there*. Ensure that your child understands the difference between these words and can use them accurately and confidently.

Punctuation practice

Name these **punctuation marks**.

, comma

: colon

; semicolon

– hyphen

" speech mark or inverted commas

! exclamation mark

Now rewrite the text below, **punctuating** it correctly and breaking it into **paragraphs**.

giants have been the main characters in fairy tales myths and legends for centuries they have been imaginary figures of fear and fun throughout the world from the west to the east and from the north pole to the south pole some have strange names like polyphemus the cyclops from greece blunderbore from england and jotun from scandinavia in many traditional stories giants who smell trouble will often thunder fee fi fo fum they are not always very clever so small cunning heroes can trick them and escape from their clutches

Giants have been the main characters in fairy tales, myths and legends for centuries. They have been imaginary figures of fear and fun throughout the world, from the West to the East and from the North Pole to the South Pole. Some have strange names like Polyphemus the Cyclops from Greece, Blunderbore from England and Jotun from Scandinavia.

In many traditional stories, giants who smell trouble will often thunder "Flee-fi-fo-fum!". They are not always very clever, so small, cunning heroes can trick them and escape from their clutches.

As your child identifies each of the punctuation marks, ask him or her to explain when and how they are used. Look closely at your child's handwriting, and point out any areas that need more practice.

Reading and understanding

Read the text below, then answer the questions in **full sentences**.

People used to believe that in ancient times Great Britain was populated by a race of giants. In legendary tales, giants are sometimes linked with particular places. Some stories about giants were originally told to explain how certain features of the landscape came to exist.

In Northern Ireland an amazing formation of thousands of columns of basalt, an igneous rock, is known as The Giant's Causeway.

Some people think that the Gog Magog Hills in Cambridgeshire, England, take their name from two legendary giants, Gog and Magog, who were said to be buried in the area.

Another story tells how The Wrekin, a hill in another part of England, was first formed when an angry giant cast down a huge spadeful of rocks and soil.

Why did people tell stories about giants?
People told stories about giants because they used to believe that in ancient times Great Britain was populated by a race of giants.

Where is The Giant's Causeway?
The Gaint's Causeway is in Northern Ireland.

How might the Gog Magog Hills have got their name?
The Gog Magog Hills might have got their names from the two legendry giants, Gog and Magog, who are said to be buried nearby.

What is the Wrekin?
The Wrekin is a hill in England.

Which of these places would you like to visit, and why?
Answers may vary

This activity provides practice in reading and comprehending information text. Make sure your child realises that the answers to all the questions can be found in the text. Ensure that your child writes his or her answers in complete sentences.

Silent w

In the passage about giants on page 12, the hill called The Wrekin has a silent **w**. All the words below also begin with a silent **w**. Add the missing letters, then use each word in a sentence of your own. D

w _r_ estle   w _r_ iting   w _r_ iggle

w _r_ en   w _r_ ing   w _r_ ong

w _r_ inkle   w _r_ eath   w _r_ ote

Answers may vary

Do you know or can you find any more words that begin with **wr-**? Make a list here. D

Answers may vary

These activities focus on the spelling of words beginning with the silent-letter combination *wr-*. Point out to your child that it is the *w* that is not pronounced. Discuss other silent letter spellings, such as words beginning with *kn-* and *gn-*.

A traditional story

Many **myths**, **legends** and **traditional stories** from around the world are about such things as fire, water, rain, wind or thunder and lightning. Sometimes these things take the form of giants, gods or spirits that can harm or help humans. Carefully read the following **information** about Norse gods.

Thor and Sif

What Thor was like

Thor was an exaggerated, colourful character. He was huge, even for a god, and incredibly strong. He had wild hair and beard and a temper to match. He was never angry for long, though, and easily forgave people. Thor raced across the sky in his chariot drawn by two giant goats, **Toothgnasher** and **Toothgrinder**. It was their hooves that people heard when it thundered on Earth. He controlled the thunder and lightning and brewed up storms by blowing through his beard. Sailors prayed to him for protection from bad weather.

Thor's magic weapons

Thor had a belt which doubled his strength when he buckled it on and iron gauntlets which allowed him to grasp any weapon. The most famous of Thor's weapons was his hammer, **Mjollnir**. It always hit its target and returned to Thor's hands after use. When a thunderbolt struck Earth, people said that Thor had flung down his hammer.

Mjollnir did not only do harm, though. It also had protective powers and people wore small copies of it as jewellery to keep them safe and bring good luck.

Sif

Thor was married to **Sif**, who was famous for her pure gold, flowing hair. She was a goddess of fruitfulness and plenty. Her hair reminded people of a field of ripe corn and the harvest.

In one of the myths her hair was cut and stolen. Her misery until the hair was replaced represented the darkness of the winter season, when the corn did not grow.

Sif and Thor lived in a great hall in Asgard, called **Bilskirnir**, which means Lightning.

From *The Usborne Book of Greek and Norse Legends*

Underline any words in the **extract** above that you do not understand, then look up their meanings in a dictionary. D

On this page, your child reads information text about thunder and lightning myths from another culture. Suggest that your child reads the passage aloud or, if your child needs more help, you could read it together.

Understanding the story

Use **full sentences** to answer these questions about the **information** on page 14.

How did the Norse people explain the sound of thunder?
The Norse people explained the sound of thunder as the sound of the two giant goats that pulled Thor's chariot.

What did the people say had happened when lightning struck Earth?
When lightning struck Earth, people said that Thor had flung down his hammer.

What happened on Earth when Thor blew through his beard?
When Thor blew through his beard, he brewed up storms on Earth.

Why did the Norse sailors pray to Thor?
The Norse sailors prayed to Thor for protection from bad weather.

What was magical about Thor's belt and gloves?
Thor's belt doubled his strength when he buckled it on, and his gloves allowed him to grasp any weapon.

Why were copies of Mjollnir worn as jewellery?
Copies of Mjollnir were worn as jewellery to keep people safe and to bring good luck.

Why was Sif famous?
Sif was famous for her pure gold, flowing hair.

What did Sif's unhappiness at the loss of her hair represent?
Sif's unhappiness at the loss of her hair represented the darkness of the winter season.

Your child may need to reread the text on page 14 before answering these questions. Ensure that he or she writes answers in complete sentences. Accept any answers that are appropriate to the text.

An Aboriginal myth

The Aboriginal people of Australia have stories about thunder and lightning. Read the two **myths** below about thunderstorms, and answer the questions that follow.

Thunderstorms

On Melville Island it is a woman, Bumerali, who strikes the ground with her stone axes mounted on long flexible handles. These are the lightning flashes which destroy the trees and sometimes the Aborigines.

The Arnhem Land Aborigines believe that the thunder-man, Jambuwul, travels from place to place on the large cumulus clouds of the wet season, shedding the life-giving rain on the earth beneath. These thunder-clouds are also the home of tiny spirit children, the yurtus, who travel on the raindrops to descend to earth and find a human mother.

From *Dreamtime Heritage* by A. and M. J. Roberts

How does Bumerali make lightning?
Bumerali makes lightning by striking the ground with her stone axes.

Who is Jambuwul?
Jambuwul is the thunder-man, who travels from place to place on the large cumulus clouds of the wet season, shedding rain.

What are the yurtus?
The yurtus are tiny spirit children who travel on raindrops to descend to earth and find a human mother.

On this page, your child reads and examines two Aboriginal myths about thunderstorms. Either ask your child to read the passage aloud or read it together. Ensure that your child writes answers in complete sentences.

Another Aboriginal myth

Read this Aboriginal **myth** about fire, and answer the questions that follow.

The Capture of Fire

Goodah, a noted magician, captured a piece of lightning as it struck a dead tree during a storm. He imprisoned it as a convenient way to make fire for his own use, and ignored demands that he share this wonderful discovery. At last the tribe became so enraged with Goodah that a group of elders called up a whirlwind just as Goodah had made a fire with his piece of lightning. The whirlwind picked up the fire and scattered it all over the country, and fire became common property when members of the tribe picked up enough burning wood to make fires for themselves.

To escape the jeers and laughter of the tribe, Goodah fled to the hills to sulk, and to plan revenge.

From *Dreamtime Heritage* by A. and M. J. Roberts

How would you describe Goodah's behaviour?

Goodah's behaviour was very selfish towards the other members of the tribe.

What does **common property** mean?

Common property means that something belongs to everyone, not just one or a few people.

Do you think Goodah was right to feel angry with the tribe for calling up a whirlwind?

Another Aboriginal myth is presented on this page. Talk about the story together. What does your child think of Goodah's behaviour? Accept any answers that are appropriate to the text.

A scientific explanation

Here is a **scientific description** of the causes of thunder and lightning.

Thunder and Lightning

Thunderclouds are huge and awesomely powerful. Very big thunderclouds tower 16 km (10 miles) or more into the air and contain enough energy to light a small town for a year. No wonder then, that they can unleash such devastating storms.

It takes very strong updraughts of air to build such huge and powerful clouds, which is why they tend to form along "cold fronts", or over ground heated by strong sunshine. Violent air currents sweep up and down outside the cloud, tearing the water droplets and ice crystals apart and then crashing them together again. These collisions load the cloud particles with static electricity – just as rubbing a balloon on a pullover does. Lightning is the sudden release of the charge built up on millions of particles within the thundercloud.

A flash of lightning heats the air along its path so dramatically that it expands at supersonic speed. This expansion causes a deafening crash of thunder.

From *How the Earth Works* by John Farndon

How is static electricity formed in clouds?

Static electricity is formed when violent winds sweep up and down clouds, tearing water droplets and ice crystals apart and then crashing them together again.

What happens when static electricity is released?

When static electricity is released a flash of lightning occurs.

Find words that could be used in *Thunder and Lightning* in place of the words below. T D

| huge | enormous | awesomely | amazingly |
| unleash | release | deafening | loud |

This page features a scientific description of thunderstorms. Point out to your child that this explanation is not more "correct" than the myths, but is a different type of writing. Any suitable alternative words are acceptable as answers to the last question.

Types of writing

Reread the **information** about Thor and Sif on page 14, the Australian Aboriginal **myths** on pages 16 and 17, and the modern **scientific explanation** of thunder and lightning on page 18. Then place the following numbered statements under the correct headings below.

1 Lightning is the release of static electricity.
2 Thunderclouds can be more than 16 km (10 miles) high.
3 Lightning is Thor's hammer.
4 Thunder is the sound of giant goats' hooves in the sky.
5 Thunder is the sound of rapidly heating air expanding.
6 Thunder comes from the thunder-man, who travels on the clouds.
7 Rain gives life to things on earth.
8 Raindrops carry tiny spirits.
9 Devastating storms often accompany thunder and lightning.
10 Thor brews up storms by blowing through his beard.
11 Fire is precious to humans.
12 Selfish behaviour is bad.
13 Sharing with others is good.

Norse legend	Aboriginal myths	Scientific explanation
Statement 3	Statement 6	Statement 1
Statement 4	Statement 7	Statement 2
Statement 10	Statement 8	Statement 5
	Statement 11	Statement 9
	Statement 12	
	Statement 13	

Ask your child to consider the list of statements on the theme of thunderstorms. Help him or her to determine the correct information source for each one. It may help if your child looks back at the relevant pages to check his or her answers.

Planning your own story

Reread the **myth** on page 17. On a separate sheet of paper, write notes on how Goodah found fire. Decide what Goodah did next. How will you end the story? Plan your story on this page by writing short notes. Decide who you will be writing your story for.

Remember: You do not need to use full sentences when writing notes.

Characters: ....

Setting: ....

Beginning: ....

What happens: ....

Ending: ....

Learning how to plan a story will improve your child's writing and increase his or her confidence. When checking the plan, make sure that he or she understands that full sentences and "best" handwriting are not needed when making notes.

Your own traditional tale

Look over the notes you wrote on page 20, then write your story here.
Remember: Use **paragraphs** for each different idea.

The Capture of Fire, and Goodah's Revenge

....
....
....
....
....
....
....
....
....
....
....
....
....
....
....
....
....
....
....
....
....
....

Answers may vary

The task on this page is to write an ending to a traditional story. Listen to your child read his or her completed story aloud. Discuss its content and structure together. Say what you admire about your child's creative writing.

Patterns in poems

Read the following **poem** aloud, then answer the questions.

> Who has seen the wind?
> Neither I nor you:
> But when the leaves hang trembling
> The wind is passing thro'.
>
> Who has seen the wind?
> Neither you nor I:
> But when the trees bow down their heads
> The wind is passing by.
>
> Christina Rossetti

How many **verses** (or stanzas) are there in this poem?

The poem has 2 verses (or stanzas).

Find the **rhyming pairs** of words in the poem. Write them here.

you – thro', I – by

Read aloud the poem, listen to the **rhythm** and count the **syllables**.
Write the number of **syllables** in each line of the poem here.

line 1 ___5___   line 2 ___5___   line 3 ___7/8___   line 4 ___6___

line 5 ___5___   line 6 ___5___   line 7 ___8___   line 8 ___6___

Write your own poem about another type of weather in the same style.

....
....

Answers may vary

Here, your child learns to recognise and appreciate different forms of poetry. Point out that while both poems are about the wind, they were written by different poets. Encourage your child to read with expression and to listen for the words that rhyme.

Haiku and cinquain

Read these two **poems** aloud.

Haiku
Poem in three lines:
Five syllables, then seven,
Five again; no rhyme.

Eric Finney

Cinquain
Cinquain:
A short verse form
Of counted syllables …
And first devised by Adelaide
Crapsey.

Gerard Benson

Write your own **haiku** about wind.
Remember to use the correct number of **syllables** in each line.

Wind

syllables: 5 ....
            7 ....
            5 ....

Answers may vary

Now write a **cinquain**. Use the same number of **syllables** in each line as in the **cinquain** above.

Wind

syllables: 2 ....
            4 ....
            6 ....
            8 ....
            2 ....

Answers may vary

On this page, the task is for your child to write two poems following the forms of a haiku and a cinquain. The most important point for your child to understand is that both poems have a set number of syllables in each line.

Soft c and homophones

All the **definitions** below are of words that begin with **ci-**. The letter **c** sounds like an **s** when these words are spoken. Use a **dictionary** to help you find the words that fit the **definitions**. D

a drink made from apples _cider_
a partly burned fuel such as coal _cinder_
a character in a fairy tale _Cinderella_
where films are shown _cinema_
a spice _cinnamon_
a shape _circle_
the distance round a circle _circumference_
a travelling show _circus_
a large town _city_
polite _civil_

The words below sound the same, but are spelt differently and have different meanings. They are called **homophones**.

great and grate   paws, pores and pause   rain, rein and reign

Can you find a **homophone** for each of these words?

awe	ore	bear	bare
ceiling	sealing	draft	draught
eight	ate	fare	fair
guest	guessed	hare	hair
inn	in	bye	by
wait	weight	sea	see
pare	pair	feet	feat

Ensure that your child knows that the letter *c* can sometimes sound like *s*. Can your child think of any more words with the soft *c* sound? The second exercise looks at homophones. Help your child find homophones for all the words in the list.

Protest letter

Read this **letter** from the *Letters to the Editor* section of a local **newspaper**, then answer, in **full sentences**, the following questions.

> Sir,
> I wish to protest, on behalf of the B.B.G. (Ban the By-pass Group), about the proposed building of a road through Birnam Wood, which was reported in last Friday's *Dunsinane Express.*
> The loss to the public of this local beauty spot and the damage to the wildlife that depends upon it would be huge.
> The wood has been allowed to grow and flourish, largely undisturbed by man, for almost one thousand years.
> Surely we, as local guardians of the environment, cannot allow the road builders to destroy this priceless piece of our natural history?
> M. Duncan (address supplied)

Why was this **letter** written?

This letter was written to object to the planned building
of a road through Birnam Wood.

In which **paragraphs** does the writer give reasons for his protest? What are his reasons?

In paragraphs 2, 3 and 4 the writer sets out the environmental issues that
form the reasons for his protest.

Why does the writer end with a **question**?

The writer ends with a question to make people think about the issue, but
he expects people to agree with him.

Do you think this **letter** will help stop the wood from being destroyed? If yes, how? If no, why not?

Answers may vary

The questions on this page help your child to assess and debate an argument. Discuss both sides of the argument with your child, and help him or her to decide whether or not the protest will be successful.

Plan an argument

Do you support or disagree with the letter on page 25? Gather together some **facts**, **opinions** and **persuasive** words so that you can plan your own **letter**. It may help to look in **reference books**, or on the **Internet**. Make some **notes** here.

Facts about trees and the environment

Answers may vary

My opinion and feelings

Answers may vary

Useful words to persuade people [D] [T]

Greed, devastation,

Answers may vary

On this page, your child prepares notes that will help him or her present a persuasive argument (on page 27). The notes should be brief and need not be in full sentences. Once your child has written the notes, discuss his or her opinions.

Letter to the newspaper

Read over your **notes** on page 26, then write your own **letter** to the newspaper about the by-pass discussed on page 25.

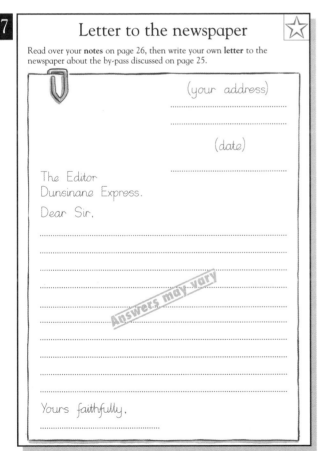

(your address)

(date)

The Editor
Dunsinane Express.

Dear Sir,

Answers may vary

Yours faithfully,

This writing activity takes the form of a formal letter aimed at a specific audience. Your child should use the notes he or she made on page 26 as a guide. Discuss the effectiveness of your child's presentation of the argument, and praise his or her efforts.

Write an explanation

Imagine that you have to **explain** what a banana is and where it comes from to someone who has never seen or heard of one. Write your **explanation** below. You may need to find out a few extra **facts** before you begin. [D]

Answers may vary

After you have written your **explanation**, turn this page upside down, and check whether your **explanation** includes any of the information given below.

A banana is an edible tropical fruit. It is finger-shaped and has a yellow skin when ripe. We usually peel off the skin and eat the pulpy inside, which is creamy white in colour.
Bananas grow in clusters on tree-like plants. They are grown in Africa, Asia, the West Indies and Latin America and are exported all over the world.

This activity provides practice in writing clear explanations. Encourage your child to think carefully before writing and to use reference material. Compare the result with the upside-down example, and comment on the similarities and differences between the two.

Instructions

A banana split is a dessert made with ice cream and a split banana. Other ingredients may be added as decoration. Write **instructions** for making a banana split. (You may need to look them up in a recipe book.) These words may be useful: peel, half/halved, lengthways, pile, decorate. **Remember:** Begin with an **introduction** that lists the ingredients, and then continue with short, **numbered statements** in the right order. D

On this page, your child can practise writing clear instructions in a particular style. He or she might like to use another recipe as an example of how to set out the text. Check that your child has put the instructions in a logical order and that they are easy to follow.

Make a point

Here is a list of ideas for a piece of **writing** about travel in towns and cities.

Improved public transport would make our towns and cities safer places.
Travel in towns and cities is sometimes slow and difficult.
Pedestrians and cyclists have to breathe polluted air.
Public transport reduces air pollution.
Private cars carry only a few people.
Buses and trains can carry many people.
Many towns and cities are too noisy and dirty.
Cars carrying a few people can cause traffic jams.
Walking and cycling are good exercise.
Public transport saves fuel.

Sort these **points** into a sensible order by giving each one a number. Then use the **points** to write one or two **paragraphs** about travel in towns and cities.

This activity encourages your child to form an argument by putting a list of ideas into a meaningful order. There can be more than one correct answer. Check that your child has arranged the ideas in a sensible order that develops to make a point.

Onomatopoeia

The words below have **sounds** that match their meanings.
Remember: When the sound of a word connects with its meaning, it is called **onomatopoeic**.

splash crash smash clash

clatter plop clap

gurgle snap buzz rumble

tinkle click whir tick

bang roar squeal

Match the **sound words** above to the different situations below. Write the relevant **sound word** in the appropriate box. Add some more **sound words** of your own if you wish!

Thunderstorm crash, splash, smash, clash, plop, gurgle, snap, rumble, bang, roar   *Answers may vary*

Sports day clap, buzz, bang, roar, squeal   *Answers may vary*

In the swimming pool splash, clatter, plop, gurgle   *Answers may vary*

In the kitchen splash, clatter, plop, tinkle, tick, whir, click   *Answers may vary*

The activity on this page revises your child's understanding of onomatopoeia. Check his or her choices for each box, and comment on any further words he or she has suggested, discussing how appropriate they are and if they are spelt correctly.

Word game

Follow the rules below to make as many words as you can from the word **TRANSPORT**.

Follow these rules:
- for each word that you make, you can use a letter as many times as it appears in the word **TRANSPORT**. This means that you can use **T** and **R** twice in a word, but all the other letters only once
- words of **fewer than three letters** do not count
- **names** of people and places do not count
- each word must be in a **dictionary** D
- each word scores **one point**

Total points ....

(15–20 good, 20–25 very good, over 25 excellent!)

This game allows your child to revise earlier work on spelling patterns and to improve spelling skills. It might help to set a time limit for this activity. You could also ban plurals as answers. Try this game with other words. Have fun!